Dark Psychology Protection

How to Analyze and Read People to Handle and Protect Your Self from Toxic People Who Use Dark NLP, Manipulation, Mind Games and Deception

Ben Partell

Table of Contents

Introduction

Chapter1: Understanding Dark Psychology/NLP

What Is Dark Psychology

What Is NLP

Uses of NLP

The Programming Aspect Of NLP

Specifics About NLP

History and Why Do People Use NLP

Human Psychology and Behavior

Who Uses Dark Psychology to Influence People?

Chapter2: How to Spot Manipulation

General Signs of Manipulation

Character Traits of a Dark Person

How to Escape Manipulation

Chapter 3: Manipulation

What Is Manipulation and How it Works

Why Do People Use Manipulation?

Examples of Manipulation

How To Deal With Manipulation

Chapter4: Mind Games/Control

What Are Mind Games

Why Do People Use Mind Control?

Examples of Mind Control in Real Life

How to Deal With It

What Is Hypnosis

Why Do People Use Hypnosis?

Examples of Hypnosis and Deception

Chapter 5: The Dark Triad

Understanding Mental Disorders

The Top 7 Mental Disorders

Narcissism

Characteristics of Narcissists

Machiavellianism

Characteristics Of Machiavellianism

Psychopathy

Chapter6: How to Read and Analyze People

How to Read People

Body Language

Human Behavior

Certain Words

Be Specific

Chapter 7: Understanding Your Identity

Rules of Mindfulness Meditation

The Voice Inside Our Head and How We Can Overcome It for the Better

How to Practice Love and Kindness Meditation

Your Inside Voice Knows Dark Psychology Inside Out

Dwelling on the Past

How to Deal with Negative Past

Acknowledge and Turn it Into Positivity

Do Something About It

Chapter 8: Toxic Friendships and Relationships

Signs a Friend or Partner Is Manipulating You

Dealing With it, and Fixing It

Conclusion

Introduction

Thank you for choosing to purchase Dark Psychology Protection. You are clearly among the many people who are on the lookout to protect themselves against manipulation. You do not have to wait until you face manipulation before you start protecting yourself. It is wise to gain knowledge and use it to protect yourself from dark psychology. Purchasing this book is the first step towards being an individual who is aware of all the danger that lurks around. You need to protect yourself and your family from people who use dark psychology techniques to gain control.

The views and concepts in this book do not, in any way, represent the final professional opinion on the subject. It is only fair that you understand this book is based on researched data and does not, in any way, represent a counseling course for dark psychology victims. You can infer to the content of this book for knowledge about the subject. You can use this knowledge for personal growth and family use.

This book is built in a systematic order, starting from the known to the unknown. Even if you have never heard about dark psychology, the book breaks down the topic in a simple way, making it easy for you to understand. The book focuses on key topics such as manipulation techniques and how they work. You will understand the commonly used manipulation techniques such as NLP and hypnosis. This book opens your eyes to how much a single individual can control your life and even control your actions through techniques such as hypnosis. This book covers each of the topics discussed in detail, breaking the points to the most basic level where you can understand.

The book is not only based on the theoretical explanation of dark psychology, but it is the most practical guide you will come across. You will get to learn practical ways of avoiding manipulation. You will look at the practical ways of avoiding manipulative people and how to ensure that you stay safe. The actions you can take are clearly outlined to help you stand outside the manipulation window. This book will help you gain some kind of immunity against manipulation.

As you enjoy reading the book, keep in mind the fact that you may also use manipulation yourself to grow in life. As much as dark psychology can be used to blackmail your life, you can also use it to blackmail other people. If you choose to use dark psychology to blackmail people and gain whatever you wish in life, you will be at a good place to experience success. As we delve into the details, follow keenly to pick everything you need for your life and for self-protection.

Chapter1: Understanding Dark Psychology/NLP

You do not write your life with words. You write it with actions. What you think is not important. It is only important what you do. Patrick Ness

If you wish to protect yourself from dark psychology, you have to understand how it works. The human mind works in an amazing way, and there are many details of the human psychology that you must understand. You may be shocked to realize that you personally have some tendencies of darkness. Understanding these tendencies and how they manifest is the first step towards living a life that is free of predators. Those who target your life should find you prepared. When you learn these facts, you can put on a shield and start protecting yourself from all individuals who intend to hurt you or break your spirit.

What Is Dark Psychology

Dark psychology basically refers to the study of the psychological nature of human beings to prey on one another. Psychology shows that all human beings have a tendency of preying on one another with the intention to do harm for self-gain. This is something that has manifested among humans since time immemorial. This behavior does not only affect humans but also affects other animals. Other animals have a tendency to intentionally want to hurt each other without specific treason. The difference between other animals and humans is that in most cases, humans use dark psychology for personal gain. According to Psychology Today, at least 99.9% of the instances where human beings try to harm others are motivated by personal gain. However, there is a small percentage of human beings that may intend to harm others for unknown reasons.

The study of these human tendencies opens your mind to the reality of the world. You should understand the techniques that dark psychologists use and how they approach the subject if you wish to be free from manipulation. One of the most dangerous dark psychology approaches is the use of NLP.

What Is NLP

Neuro-linguistic programming -NLP refers to a set of skills used in communication that reveal what matters most on the inside through outward expression. To understand the NLP language, you must be able to relate it to your normal language to the outward expressions. An NLP expert can extract a lot of information from your normal communication by observing your actions and expressions. In NLP, you can extract information from a person's normal communication. The information extracted can help you understand the line of thinking of a person and their beliefs.

There are so many definitions of NLP that it becomes complex and difficult to understand for many people. The simplest way to understand NLP is to think of the human brain as a map. NLP outlines the human brain as a map of all the instances that the person has gone through in life. This map has specific landmarks that represent the important events that a person as gone through. The important life instances end up making the beliefs that a person anchors their life upon. NLP teaches you how to spot the important landmarks in a person's mind. When you talk to a person, you can recognize their beliefs and their thoughts by extracting important information from their words. To understand NLP, we have to look at each of these words and their distinctive meaning (Neuron, Linguistic and programming)

Uses of NLP

NLP has many uses, and dark manipulation is not on the top of the list. Matter of fact, NLP is used for personal growth and self-improvement.

If you want to become a better version of yourself, you can use some of the techniques above to reprogram your mind. Through visualization, you can easily change your negative perceptions of life and start observing it in a positive light. It is important to note that NLP is designed for self-growth and can help you restore your self-esteem and improve your thinking process.

NLP is used to promote skills such as self-reflection, communication, confidence, among others. You can use NLP to achieve work-oriented goals and see success in your relationships with others. If you implement the techniques right, you will gather influence as a leader and easily rise to a position of power within your work environment.

With that said, it is also relevant to mention the dark side of NLP. The fact that the language can lead to a total reprogramming of a person's mind is a big risk. The fact that through NLP, you can learn about a person's beliefs and be able to influence them makes it a dangerous tool. If you want to practice NLP, you should have the intention of progress. Your main target should be growth and improved productivity. You must reduce your selfish ambitions and focus on the common good of the majority. You can use NLP to help the individuals you work with or the people who work below you realize their full potential. You can also use NLP to improve your personal performance and your socialization with other people within your firm.

NLP is also applied in medical terms, especially when dealing with mental conditions. It can be used to help individuals suffering from anxiety and depression. Most such individuals only experience worry, fear, and panic attacks due to associating past events with some triggers. Through the NLP approach, you can help such individuals change their emotional associations. You can help them start associating certain circumstances with positivity and not negativity. The sensory association on certain triggers may help patients of anxiety and depressions improve their general outlook on life.

NLP has also been found to be helpful for PTSD patients. Any person that has gone through traumatic events in life may have a very unrealistic approach to life. Negativity becomes a constant part of the life of such individuals. If you learn to use NLP, you can bond with such individuals, extract the right information, and use it to reprogram the minds of the person you are targeting.

The Programming Aspect Of NLP

Neuron: This refers to the brain and how the state of mind affects the body. NLP as a language will teach you how to relate a person's behavior to their state of mind at a particular time. As you become an NLP expert, you will find it easier to associate the actions of a person to their thoughts or state of mind.

Linguistic: Linguistic refers to the language of communication. In NLP, our bodies and mind reveal what we are saying even without saying it loud with words. With NLP, you have to be an expert in observation. Through outward observation of a person's actions and behavior, you should be able to fish out plenty of information. NLP teaches us how to access unconscious information that might have remained unknown to us otherwise. In normal communication, we only observe and note conscious information. Conscious information can be communicated through words or expressions. However, in NLP, the unconscious information passes right in front of your face, and you may never notice it unless you choose to look beyond the conscious.

Programming: Programming mainly refers to changing the thought process and the response of a person to certain issues. A person who has been trained in NLP is programmed to study and understand the mental programming of other people. Through NLP, a person can observe the habitual thoughts and feelings of another person. If you are an NLP expert, you can observe the actions and reactions of a person and be in a position to interpret their thoughts and actions without speaking a word. A good example of programming is in a case where you ask someone a question. You can learn a lot from a person just by observing their visual and audio aspects when they answer the question.

For example, if you ask a person- What is the color of your car? There are two approaches that the person can use. If the person turns their eyes to the upper right corner when answering the question, they have visually created the color of the car. However, if the person answers by turning the eye to the upper left corner of the eye, they have visually remembered the color of the eye. NLP programming goes into the detail of understanding a person. Through such programming, the expert can understand the thoughts of a person and can even see lies without you speaking. In our example above, the person who turns their eye to the upper left corner is creating color in their mind. In other words, they are either lying, or they do not have a car at all.

Specifics About NLP

According to Mehrabian (1972), words are the least meaningful part of a conversation, only accounting for 7% of the information being communicated. If you are an individual who only pays attention to words in a conversation, the chances are that you only get 7% of the conversation. When someone is talking to us, it is common to ask questions such as what does he mean? Such questions can only get answers by observing the other aspects of the communicator. For instance, if a person tells you, I will see you tomorrow, but their voice is flat and their eyes focused on something else, chances are that you may never see that person tomorrow. The words that come out of the mouth of a person should relate to body actions. If they do not relate, the communication process is suffering a bridge. NLP teaches you to link and combine the body language with the words spoken.

To understand the 93% of communication that escapes a person's words, you need to have some basic NLP skills. This means that you should be able to extract data from a person without paying attention to words. Just by looking and observing the facial expressions, paying attention to the voice and intonation, and observing bodily action, you can extract a lot of information about a person. This information is more accurate and relevant than the information relayed out through words.

To understand NLP, you must think of communication as a much more complex process than just passing information between two individuals. The largest percentage of communication happens within a person. This type of inner communication plays an important role in understanding people. Inner communication entails feelings, attitude, and mindset, among others. All these forms of communication play an important role in determining your actions and your words. NLP is based on internal communication; any person who wishes to understand the dark side of humanity must be in a position to observe and understand the inner communications of the people around them. If you wish to protect your life from the dark part of the world, you must be able to understand the language of communication used within the mind of a person. You should be able to look at a person and interpret what they think even before they speak.

For example, if you are hosting a party at home and you have friends over, then it turns out that you are feeling tense, you may try to hide your anxiety. Although you may tell all the people around to feel welcomed and enjoy themselves, an NLP expert can tell that you are tense. When you are an NLP expert, you pay attention to physiological and physical emotional expressions. You can look at a person and see that they are not behaving as they would if they were in a normal state of mind. The mind and the body are in constant communication. This communication helps you understand what is going on in the real world.

History and Why Do People Use NLP

NLP is a very new subject, although it has received so much public attention. You may think that it is something that has been around for centuries. In reality, the study of NLP only started in the 1970s. In 1972, in Santa Cruz California a 20-year-old psychology student Richard Bandler at U.C Santa Cruz, became friends with an associate professor of linguistics at the university Dr. John Grinder. Dr. John Grinder and Richard started a relationship that led them to explore human behavior in several aspects. Although Richard was a computer science student at the time, he changed his interests and chose to focus on human psychology.

Bandler decided to approach the subject of human behavior based on computer models. This is the reason why NLP is known as the product of computer programming and linguistics. He first modeled the methods used by Virgina Stir, an American Author and social worker. Later on, Bandler modeled the work of another psychotherapist Fritz Perls that was centered around gestalt therapy. These models also helped in the development of NLP.

In their modeling, Richard and John only had the aim of defining the methods used by psychologists in understanding human behavior. As they modeled different approaches used by psychologists, they gained a deeper understanding of the subject. Eventually, they developed NLP, which was a model based on the study of unconscious communication. Other authors and psychologists started contributing to the models and eventually allowed the concept to fully develop.

Although the concept of NLP is widely accepted, it is also widely criticized. It is important to look at NLP with an open mind. Although it has so many positives when it comes to understanding the human behavior, some negatives make it a bit complex for the common person. It is only those who have deep programming knowledge and human psychology understanding who can use NLP to the fullest.

Unless you have some experience or have undergone specialized training, you may not be in a position to understand or use NLP effectively. This is the weak point of the language. With that said, you can learn NLP and use it for your benefit.

Human Psychology and Behavior

Psychologists have spent so much time trying to study and understand human behavior. To some extent, they have managed to unravel the factors that make human beings behave in the ways they do. However, there are still many factors that stand out as a mystery. NLP tries to answer questions that are very key to understanding the dark side of the human mind. Very few people are comfortable with the fact that a human being can turn evil at any time and can cause harm even to the people they love. Understanding all these aspects of human behavior requires a critical analysis of human behavior and the actions of a normal human being.

Human behavior is generally anchored upon 3 key factors: desire, investment, and social influence.

Human Desire: Desire is the human push or strong urge to fulfill certain things in life. The human mind is motivated to achieve certain goals, and once the urge to achieve such goals kicks in, you cannot stop it. The desire to have something or someone pushes a person to the edge, pulling them towards doing anything necessary to see that the end goal is achieved. Although a person may not have a desire for something specific, the more they think about it, the more it manifests. If you start thinking about owning a house, your desire for the same grows by the day. However, if you already have a house, your desire to own something else will supersede the desire to own a house.

Human desire is also motivated by the environment and the social setting. As we will see later, the social environment plays an important role in defining a person's psychology. All human beings are naturally selfish. They are wired in such a way that they have to think of themselves first before thinking about another. This style of thinking drives many people into taking actions that are subconsciously dark. Although all human beings are manipulative and dark, they try to control these selfish tendencies. Some people can manage to suppress their dark sides to insignificant levels; however, this does not mean that the dark side does not exist. For instance, a mother may deny herself for the sake of the child. However, this is only possible when the environment is conducive. But when it comes to a serious situation where the mother has to choose between death and life, it is common to see the mother abandon the child.

All human beings tend to self-protect and the desire to have the best things in life. This desire pushes us to behave the way we behave. Given that we are more evolved than other animals, we have come to develop more sophisticated desires than other animals. Human beings show the strongest desires when it comes to achieving safety, territory, sex, food, and social standing. These areas of life may make a person do things that are out of control. Among the factors that drive our desires, we only share a few with other animals. Wild animals only show more desire than humans when it comes to their urge to find food and safety. Although animals may fight over sexual partners, they are a lot less sophisticated and aggressive as compared to humans.

Social influence: The other factor that matters a lot is social influence. When it comes to controlling human behavior, you need to think about social influence. Social influence refers to factors that are drawn from peers and society at large. Aristotle noted that the human being is an incredibly social animal. One of the most important aspects of human-environment is people. Human psychology and behavior are deeply anchored upon the environment. If you stay in an environment without people, your behaviors might be very different from what they are when there are people around. This explains why early human beings did not pay so much attention to sophistication. They lived a simple life and did not even have a desire to dress up or look good. However, as human beings develop, the world's social environment also develops. The people around you push you to desire a better life.

Human psychology observes that all human beings pay attention to the words and opinions of others. Every person has a desire to be seen as successful, beautiful, and important in society. Such desires that link back to what the people around us think can drive us to do anything. People have undergone plastic surgery just to look appealing to the people around them. Due to the need for approval from the social class, people go to all extends to look for money, beauty, and other accessories that the society deems relevant and important. Anything that is deemed important in a certain society must be a cause for contention. It attracts the strongest desire and is the only way to observe the true human behavior.

Investment: Every human being works so hard to achieve their desired goals. The push to fulfill desire leads to investment. When a person makes an investment, they attach value to it. Trying to take away any investment of a person may lead you to the dark side of a person. If you wish to see the true colors of a person, try touching something they value.

Value in the human mind is either economic or sentimental. In either case, a person has to invest in terms of time, effort, and finances. For instance, if a person invests money in a business, they will go to all extends to protect the same business. The same also applies to relationships. If you invest so much time in a relationship, you will go to all extends to protect your relationship. These aspects of a human being show the value that a person attaches to investment. Any activity that costs energy requires that you protect the outcome.

Interestingly, you cannot spot the true characteristics of any person by observing their conscious actions. For many people, the true person hides in the subconscious.

Freudian theorists claim that conscious beliefs and desires play a very small role in unraveling the personality of a person. In reality, the true character of a person hides in the subconscious. There are several reasons why a person may hide their true nature in the subconscious. One reason is that the human mind is trained to show the best part of a person. As mentioned, all human beings strive to suppress the dark side. In other words, although a person may have a dark side, they may not show it outwardly. In some cases, even a dark person may not think that they have a dark side. Most people like to think of themselves as being good people. It is only until you try their patience by touching something they value that you see the true character of a person coming out.

Who Uses Dark Psychology to Influence People?

You might be thinking that you do not have to learn dark psychology because you do not have the intention to control people. While this might be true, it is important to learn dark psychology. In reality, we do not learn dark psychology so that we can control people. We only learn dark psychology so that we may protect ourselves from manipulative individuals. Even if you do not learn dark psychology, you will still encounter dark people. Although all human beings are dark to some extent, there are those who have an extreme level of evil in their system. There are individuals who are constantly looking for another person to hurt. You must protect yourself from such individuals, by being able to read their thoughts and intentions even before they start talking to you.

There are several groups of people who thrive in using dark psychology to control others. You need to protect yourself from such. Some of the people who use dark psychology include:

Competitors at the workplace: You might be thinking that there is a special group of people who employ dark psychology techniques. The reality is that all people are dark. If you are keen, you should have noticed that even your mother might use dark psychology to control your life. The most common cases of dark psychology occur in the workplace. This is because there is a motive for success. Since all people have a desire to succeed in whatever they do, people will go to all extends to gain control at the workplace. You must be very careful at your workplace if you hold a high position. In most cases, dark psychologists target high positions. The dark psychologist knows that if he/she can get in your mind and extract information through techniques such as NLP, he/she might have a strong reason to control your life. One thing that you must learn is to hide any information pertaining to your desires. Unless you can hide any relevant data about your personality, you may end up suffering in the hands of manipulators.

Political leaders: Another group of individuals who use dark psychology is political leaders. Politicians will go to all extends to gain power and influence. One of the biggest motives for dark psychology is having influence. If a person wants to control your life, they will strive to gain power and influence. Political leaders learn the art of mass control by using dark psychology techniques such as brainwashing and persuasion. When they learn about your weaknesses, they can use the same weakness to come against you. They use dark psychology to discredit their opponents and use manipulation to control the voters.

Controlling relationship partners: The other group of people that thrives in using dark psychology entails controlling partners. Some individuals only feel comfortable if they are the heads of a relationship. They work hard to see that they take charge of the relationship. If you happen to be in a relationship with a person who loves to be in control, you should be very careful. Such people will go to all extents to ensure that they control the relationship. A controlling relationship partner does not allow you the freedom to make choices. They will use techniques such as NLP to learn about your personality and use the same techniques to try and control your actions. If a person can study and master your ways, it is easy for such a person to control your life. Dark psychologists use NLP to capture your thoughts.

They first understand your operations and way of life and use it directly against you.

Chapter2: How to Spot Manipulation

Given that there are plenty of people out there trying to manipulate your life and control your life choices, you must learn how to spot manipulation. You should be able to tell whether a person is trying to control your actions and thinking process. Most manipulators are very cunning. They will not show their intentions outwardly. When a manipulative person comes to you, they come with the best intentions. They try to show you that they care and that they cannot hurt you. This is the reason why you have to pay more attention to subconscious cues during conversations. People do not always mean what they say.

General Signs of Manipulation

Codependency development: The first step that any manipulative person develops is codependency. Before a manipulative person starts using their tactics to break you down or to force you to do something, they will first make sure you are dependent on them. Codependency is purely a psychological game that is anchored on the fact that the manipulator needs you in their life. Because the manipulator wants to gain from you, he/she must make sure that you deem the relationship beneficial. If a manipulator wants to gain from your money or your influence, they will draw you close and make you feel that you need each other in the relationship. They will create an ideal situation where you cannot live or survive with each other. Through continuous use of lies and creating scenes, the manipulator will find a way of making you believe that the relationship is important for the two of you. While this tactic may work, sooner or later, the victim may realize that they are being used. If you are in any relationship where you feel that you cannot live without the other person, the chances are that you are being manipulated. The reality is that life cannot be built around a single person. You should be able to survive in any part of the world without the fear of lacking anything just because of a single person.

Isolation: Isolation is a tactic that manipulators use in order to take the victim to a place where they do not have any help. In dark psychology, a person cannot completely manipulate you in public. It is difficult for a person to control your life and take full advantage of you if you have friends around. For this reason, most manipulators isolate the victim. Unfortunately, most victims never notice when isolation is happening. The manipulator will tell you that you are being targeted by other people. Manipulators create conflict between the victim and the victim's friends and family. Such conflict often leads to the breakup of relationships. If you are in a relationship where you have been forced to break your connection to friends or family, you should run away as quick as possible. No one should ever come in between you and your family or friends. Even if you are in love, you must make sure you maintain old relationships.

Taking you on a guilt trip: The other obvious sign of manipulation is when a person keeps taking you on guilt trips. A guilt trip includes a situation where a person makes you feel guilty even if you did not do anything wrong. Manipulators will use guilt trips to get whatever they want. A manipulative person knows that you will do anything when you are guilty. It is common for people to atone for their mistakes by pleasing the person they have wronged. If a person keeps on taking you on guilt trips, they are looking for favors. Such favors are only a way of taking advantage of you, and this is the clearest form of manipulation that you can experience.

Playing the blame game: Blame games are different from guilt trips in that when a person plays blame games, there is a reason to blame. A person who thrives in blaming others only sees you as the wrong one. In blame games, the manipulative person may even have a substantial point to prove. If you realize that you are always being blamed for a mistake in the relationship, you need to step back and examine the relationship. Although you are allowed to take responsibility for your mistakes in a relationship, you should not be the one shouldering all the blames in a relationship. There must be days when the other person takes responsibility for the mistakes that happen in your relationship.

Attack on self-esteem: The target of a manipulative person is to ensure that you doubt yourself. A manipulative person will attack your self-esteem in every way possible to make you feel as if you are not worthy. If you are in any relationship where the other party keeps on throwing insults your way, you need to examine the relationship. Manipulative individuals attack a person's self-esteem by using verbal abuse, demeaning words, and mind control tactics. It is important for you to keep a sober mind at all times if you wish to stand against manipulators. You can use your strong stand to silence the manipulators and ensure that you protect your emotions from being affected by the insults. If you allow the manipulator to affect your emotions, they may end up taking full control of your life.

Setting up traps: Other manipulators use traps to take you on guilt trips. For instance, someone may ask you a question in which he/she is trying to trap you. If a person asks you a question where any answer you give is controversial, the chances are that he is trying to set a trap for you so that they can manipulate you.

Character Traits of a Dark Person

- **Egoism**: A dark person thinks that he/she is better than other people. This is the main reason why people take selfish actions. If you think that you are better and you deserve better, you may end up hurting others just to please yourself.

- **Machiavellianism**: For a dark person, the end justifies the means. In other words, a person can do anything possible to achieve their desire. As long as the person gets whatever they want, they do not have any reason to regret it.

- **Moral disengagement:** Most dark people lose their conscience and end up living a carefree life. In most cases, such people can do unthinkable acts without feeling guilty about it. They do not pay attention to natural laws or ethics. They disregard the social norms in the society in which they live.

- **Narcissism**: They are likely to show an excessive sense of self-worth and an exaggerated ego. Most people who use dark manipulation techniques think that they are better to such an extreme extent.

-
- **Psychological entitlement:** In their minds, they believe that they are entitled to have the best things in life. They believe that because they are better than most people, they are entitled to better things than most people.

- **Psychopathy:** It is common for people who use dark manipulation to lack empathy. A person who uses dark psychology is willing to hurt people just to get whatever they want. They do not show remorse for their actions. They seem to be dead inside with impassive show of emotions even during the most extreme occasions.

How to Escape Manipulation

Understanding that manipulation is real and accepting the fact that manipulators are out there to hurt you is the first step to being able to escape the long hand of manipulation. Manipulation is a very complex subject, and understanding manipulators will help you escape manipulation. Here is a simple step by step guide on how to escape manipulation.

Step1: Study Your Relationship using NLP

Do not just look at your relationships from outside. You need to look at all the relationships you have from an internal perspective. From an internal perspective, you look at the relationship and try to spot the subconscious motive of your relationship partners. You cannot escape a manipulative relationship if you do not know its motive. This first step should help you categorize your relationship as either manipulative or non-manipulative. You can use the characteristics mentioned above to observe your relationships and try to determine which is manipulative. Look at all types of relationships, including romantic, friendships, and even family relationships. There are many cases where parents or siblings manipulate one another. Take your time to monitor all relationships while comparing them to the factors above. Compare your relationships to the signs of manipulation above. If you realize that your relationship shows more than three signs of manipulation, you need to move to the next step.

Step 2: Rebuild your relationships

If it is true that you are in a manipulative relationship, then there are high chances that you have been isolated. Only a few manipulators will try to take control of your mind without isolation. In most cases, you are isolated and made to break relationships with friends and family. If it is true that you are in a manipulative relationship, you must first rebuild broken relationships. Since the relationships are of close people, including friends and family, you can approach several old friends and try mending fences. You may also try to explain to them that you are under a manipulative relationship.

However, if you are still at the early stages of the relationship, you should stop isolation. If you realize that a person is trying to separate you from the people you have known for a long time, you should stop them. One of the best ways to stop manipulation is ensuring that you always have friends and family close. Have a person you can share your secrets with. Try explaining to such people the things that are happening in your life. If you keep your relationship open, you will enjoy a fulfilling relationship that is not manipulative in any way.

Step 3: Find help from old friends and family
Once you have rebuilt your old relationships, find help from such people. There are many reasons you will be needing these people in your life. If you are already in an advanced relationship, the chances are that the manipulative individual has taken control of your social and financial life. Manipulative individuals will lower your self-esteem and reduce you to nothing. They will take your money and sabotage your success so that they may control your life. If you wish to get out of such relationships, you will need financial help and social support. Unless you have someone who can support you in your quest to escape manipulation, you may easily find yourself walking straight back into the same relationship. For this reason, it is important to bring old friends and family on board. Talk to these people and try making them understand your current situation.

Step 4: Cut communication and move out
If you are living with a manipulative person under one roof, you have to move out. Given that you have support in all areas of your life, you are now in a position to move out of the relationship and start rebuilding your life. Ensure that you cut all forms of communication between you and the other party. If you continue communicating, the other person may pull you into the relationship and may cause you to lose track of your decision. Most people try moving out of manipulative relationships and end up being pulled back. If you are not careful, you might be pulled back into the same relationship that you were trying to escape.

Chapter 3: Manipulation

The subject of manipulation is complex, and as much as we may discuss it, t many factors that must be addressed independently. Although most people have suffered manipulation and know how it feels, only a few people can describe what manipulation is. Manipulation is the darkest aspect of human psychology. When we are looking at dark psychology and how dark people operate, the main focus is on manipulation. The darkest of all people use underhand tactics to gain influence, power, and control. Such tactics may work or may fail. However, in the long run, a manipulative person my achieve whatever they want.

What Is Manipulation and How it Works

In this book, we will be focusing on psychological manipulation. Although there are other forms of manipulation, a dark psychologist will only focus on the psychological aspect of a person when trying to use manipulation. Psychological manipulation mainly refers to a type of social influence that targets to change the thoughts and behavior of others through indirect or deceptive tactics. A manipulative person uses indirect means to make a person change their actions or thoughts. Some of the indirect tactics include persuasion and brainwashing. In persuasion, a person does not force you to do something, but they try to convince you to do it. A good example of persuasion is marketing. Although an advertisement is aimed directly at convincing you to purchase a certain item, you are not in any way forced to purchase. The choice to purchase or not to is in your hands. The only aspect that an advertiser works on is to ensure that you see the beauty of the item. The advertiser will only tell you about the good aspects of the item you are trying to buy without mentioning the negatives. Even those who chose to mention the negatives, also try to show the negatives as a positive light. This is an indirect way of luring someone into making a purchase.

Manipulation is a way of social influence into doing something you did not necessarily want to do. However, this does not mean that social influence in itself is something bad. Social influence can be used for a good cause. You can influence someone to stop taking drugs or change some unhealthy habits. When you persuade a person to do such actions, it cannot be termed as manipulation. Social influence only becomes a manipulative habit if it is aimed at benefiting the influencer. If you can persuade someone into taking another job just to benefit from their salary, you are a manipulator. Most manipulative individuals do not deem their actions harmful in any way. When a person is using manipulation tactics, he/she targets to benefit without directly being seen as a bad person. In most cases, a manipulative person will lure you into doing something bad and end up blaming you for the same. In simple terms, a manipulative individual uses other people as puppets. You are just a tool that the manipulator uses to achieve a certain goal. A manipulative person can use you to steal money and end up playing all the blame on you.

Why Do People Use Manipulation?

To gain wealth: People use manipulation to fulfill their desires in the world. If you want money, you may use any means possible to get a good job. This is a very big motivation for most people across cultures. All over the world, people use manipulation just to get wealth. Since money is a valuable asset in life— that can give you access to most of your desires, most people will do anything just to gain money. Such motives will make most people use manipulation.

To maintain their integrity: Many people use manipulation just to keep their names clean. If a person has evil intentions but does not want the world to see them, they will use manipulation. Narcissists use manipulation and blackmail to hide their weaknesses. A narcissistic person may even ruin your name in public or lower your self-esteem just to avoid showing the world that they are weak. Most people who are striving to maintain social authenticity may go to large extends in their drive to maintain social standings.

To gain influence: The other reason why people use manipulation is to gain influence. Social influence gives people power. Most people enjoy it when they have power and control over others. We have talked about the example of political leaders and how they use manipulative tactics just to gain control over the masses. Politicians will do anything possible as long as they gain control. It is normal for people to employ such tactics in their search for power and influence. A person who wants power and influence will approach you with lies and trickery just to gain power over you.

To dominate relationships: Most people feel safe when they are the dominating voice in a relationship. It is normal for human beings to want to have control over a relationship. This desire to control a relationship may make a person want to manipulate others. Manipulation will help such individuals control the relationship partner and hence gain control of the related assets. The main reason for the desire to have control is the fear of the unknown. If a person is in a relationship and does not have a clear knowledge of the future, they may use underhand methods to control the relationship.

Self-satisfaction: In some instances, the people who use manipulation are only looking for a way to satisfy their ego. Many individuals suffer low self-esteem and only find satisfaction in controlling others. You may be in a manipulative relationship trying to figure out whatever you did that was wrong. In some instances, you may do everything right but still become a victim of manipulation. People practice manipulation just to feel satisfied and happy. Such people have deeply rooted emotional and psychological issues that need to be addressed by an expert.

Examples of Manipulation

There are many real-life examples of manipulation occurring right next to you in your daily life. If you are keen enough, you may be able to notice how certain people use manipulation and blackmail to have their way in life. It is common to spot such cases in the workplace. In family situations, manipulation comes in place when there is something valuable at stake. For instance, if a wealthy person dies without leaving a clear will, there will be many people fighting to take control of the property of the deceased.

A real-life example of manipulation would be the case of Jonestown Guyana. The story of Jonestown is one of the most documented cases of manipulation and brainwashing. The mastermind behind the story being Jim Jones, who was a religious/cult leader.

Jim Jones rose to fame in Northwest Guyana during the early 70s. His rise to fame was associated with the supernatural. Like all manipulative individuals, Jones managed to gather a small group of brainwashed individuals around himself.

One of the key characteristics of manipulative individuals is isolation, as we have observed. However, manipulators who wish to gain public influence and control large crowds of people, do not only use isolation. Most public manipulators use the inner circle approach. An inner circle is made up of people who subscribe to the ideologies of the manipulator. The ideologies are often deemed as right, and they are not seen to have anything wrong. This is an approach that most cultic sects take. When a person is introduced to the inner circle, he is made to feel special, but at the same time, he is required to fulfill certain conditions. In most cases, you will find that members of the inner circle are required to pay allegiance to the leader of the sect.

Like all sects, Jim Jones started to create a small circle of people who would later work as recruiters. The entire village of Jonestown started subscribing to the ideologies and teachings of Jones. After some time, many people subscribed to the teachings. The social pressure associated with the people joining the sect attracted even more people. The more people gathered to the sect, the more manipulative the man became. In the mid-1970s, Jim Jones pronounced himself as being a god who had come to rescue the people from their predicaments. Given that the case happened at a time when people were suffering from poor economic status, the leader took advantage of the situation. The poor villagers were drawn to him in the hope that he was going to make their lives better. They gave their attention to him and allowed him to take control of all their lives.

Just like all manipulative leaders, Jim Jones did not care about the welfare of the people. He did not provide whatever he promised. Instead, he used his popularity to amass wealth from the victims. He lured the victims into giving him sexual favors and managed to control the whole village.

The story of Jim Jones climaxed with the massacre of over 900 people who followed the sect leader. The town was named after this merciless sect leader who did not bother to think about the welfare of the people. As a manipulative person, he did not mind killing 900 people just to get whatever he wanted. Although the story of Jonestown is an extreme case that looks at a person who showed sociopathic tendencies, it reveals the true character of a manipulative person. Most manipulators do not care about how you feel or what you think. They aim to gain and move on with life.

How To Deal With Manipulation

There is no doubt about the fact that you will meet manipulative people in your life. In your drive to succeed in life, you will come across people who want to use your money or those who want to ride on your back. Such individuals will use all types of manipulative tactics to try and control your life. It is important that you find a way of controlling them. Controlling manipulative persons is about ensuring that you stop them even before they start. Some of the ways to stop manipulative individuals include:

Staying observant: If you know that you are a target, you must be observant at all times. In other words, we all need to stay observant. Everybody is a prime target of manipulation. People will come to you to take advantage of your situation. Staying observant means that you can look at people and read their intentions. As we have observed, NLP professionals will use their extraction techniques to try and gauge our thoughts and beliefs. If you wish to stop such individuals from controlling your life and thinking process, you must be aware. Always try to remember that there is someone out there who may be looking to take control of your thoughts.

Be secretive: Do not be a person who gives out your information to all people. A manipulative person can only control you if they know something about you. If the manipulator does not have any information about you, he/she may not have any valid reasons to control your life. If you want to stay on your feet and stop all people who come to your life with the intention of control, you must learn to stop them by blocking their quest to gain knowledge about your walk.

Learn to control your emotions: NLP experts do not need you to speak for them to collect information. NLP experts rely more on the emotional clues that you send out during conversations. You must learn how to control your expressive and physiological aspects of emotions. The physiological aspects of emotion include the bodily changes that take place when you are emotional. For instance, the sweating of hands when you are anxious or afraid. Such physiological changes may sell you out to the person who wants to get more information in order to manipulate you. The expressive aspect of emotions includes bodily actions that you take when you are emotional. A good example would be running away when you are afraid. Although you may choose to stay, the action or running away or choosing to fight is an expressive part of your emotions that NLP experts may use to gain more information about your past.

Avoid isolation: Try as much as possible to ensure that you do not allow a manipulative person to isolate you. When you are isolated, you are weak and vulnerable. Most manipulative persons gain control during moments of weakness, such as isolation.

Chapter4: Mind Games/Control

What Are Mind Games

Mind games refer to psychological tactics that a person uses to control another person's mind by inverting reality. When a person plays mind games, they make the victim feel guilty or responsible for mistakes, or they make the victim feel inferior, stupid, embarrassed, and unworthy in public. Mind games are very dangerous because they can break down a person's esteem and make that person lose self-worth.

People who play mind games include manipulative individuals, insecure people in relationships, and people who are not mature enough for relationships. Mind games are often used to put the victim on a test or to make the victim feel guilty. Some examples of mind game tactics include:

Playing Hard to Get: This is a tactic that is used by men and women in relationships. Some business persons also use the tactic to control others. When a person plays hard to get, they may give you mixed signs. For instance, if you are chasing a woman, she might show interest but keeps on telling you no. Such a situation often sends the victim into a state of confusion and frustration.

Projecting: Projecting is a situation where a person translates their thoughts and actions to you. For example, if you are in a relationship with a person who is cheating, they may blame you for doing the same. These are mind games that are played by insecure persons to stop the victim from making the same mistakes they are already doing.

 ending Mixed Messages: A person who sends mixed messages aims at confusing your mind. For instance, a person may act interested in you today just to turn around and show a complete lack of interest in you the next day.

Guilt Tripping: Guilt-tripping is commonly used by manipulative individuals when they want to gain favors. In guilt-tripping, the manipulator will make you feel guilty even if you have done nothing wrong. In most cases, they make you feel guilty for their mistakes, or they make something normal feel like a very big mistake.

Withholding Rights: If you are in a relationship with any person, you have your rights. For instance, in a marriage situation, you have rights to sexual intimacy. When a person wants to play with your mind, they may withhold sexual favors, or they may use sexual intimacy as a reward in order to get special treatment from you.

Love Bombing: Most people do not know how to spot when they are being love-bombed. Love bombing is the first and most obvious sign of a manipulative relationship. If a person approaches you to start a relationship, and they seem so perfect and too good to be true, you must examine their intentions. During the early days of manipulative relationships, the manipulator comes in with the most impressive and romantic gestures. The manipulators seem to have a telepathic connection with the victim. This is a relationship you must examine well; otherwise, you may find yourself in the hands of a manipulative person.

Testing Limits: Testing limits is a form of mind games that can get very dangerous. A person playing mind games may do something hurtful intentionally just to test your reaction. In testing limits, a person tries to provoke your emotions just to see how far you can get when you are angry. Such mind games are emotionally painful and can cause far-reaching harm to the victim.

Why Do People Use Mind Control?

There are many reasons why people play mind games and use them to control others. Some of the main reasons why a person would engage in mind control include:

Insecurities in relationships: People who suffer from insecurities are among the most manipulative. If you look at some of the ways that a person plays mind games above, you will realize that they are mostly about insecurities. When a person feels insecure in a relationship, they use mind games to gauge whether their partner loves them or not. Mind games are also used as a trap to stop the other person from cheating. Although the person using such games to control the minds of others thinks that they are doing the right thing, the reality is that mind games and mind control are only a show of desperation.

The desire for power: People also use mind control to gain power. Tactics such as guilt-tripping and projecting are used to make a person lose credibility and as a result, surrender power. In a relationship where two parties are fighting over control of power, it is much difficult to stay without infighting.

Need to be influential: The other reason why most people get controlling is the desire to have influence in public. If a person knows that influence will give them power, they will play all types of mind games in order to gain control. This is a common tactic employed by political leaders and top managerial leaders in firms. It is common to spot such people trying to manipulate others and through playing mind games just to get people on their side.

Low self-esteem: Some people just play mind games to fulfill their low self-esteem. Low self-esteem is a situation where a person lacks confidence; as a result, they try manipulating and controlling others so that they may feel good about themselves. This is a common case among narcissistic individuals.

Mental/social disorders: Mental and social disorders include personalities such as narcissistic personality disorder, psychopathic personality disorders, and sociopaths, among others. People who suffer from such social and mental disorders may practice manipulation for self-gain or out of sheer satisfaction. Some people who suffer from mental disorders practice manipulation for totally unknown reasons.

Examples of Mind Control in Real Life

One of the most obvious cases of mind control in history is recorded from the Indian independence fight. When a person uses mind control, they can get many people to do actions that are beyond imagination. Mahatma Gandhi, the respected Indian freedom fighter, was a man who could get into the mind of any person. Through his persuasion and mind control tactics, he managed to rally large groups of Indians behind his cause, forcing the British rule to come to an end. However, unlike other freedom fighters across the world, Gandhi did not use energy or bullets to fight. He only tapped into the psychology of the Indian people. He used his words and persuasion to make the Indian people do acts that naturally drove the white man away.

Just by using manipulation, he caused a blood bath throughout India. He managed to convince people to get into mass resistance with terrible acts such as slashing their bodies. The streets of India from the capital to the villages were filled with blood. People were willing to kill themselves just to drive the white man away. Through his ability to influence and control the minds of people, he managed to get people to harm themselves.

This is how deep mind control can get. When you allow a person to get into your mind, you allow that person to have complete control over your life. It is important to note that mind controllers have different reasons. Some use mind control for a good cause. However, in most cases, mind control is about gaining power and dominance. You should be careful to the extent you allow another person to control your mind. As much as you may want to allow another person to be part of your life, you should never give a single person too much power over your life. It should not come to a point where another person can advise you to harm yourself, and you do it without asking questions. In dark psychology, hypnosis and brainwashing techniques can be used to control your actions to the extent of harming your own body. In the case of Gandhi, mind control was used for a good cause. However, the actions that took place to achieve good cause were devastating.

How to Deal With It

The fact that people will try controlling your mind does not mean that you should allow them. As much as people will come to you trying to take over and control your actions, you must learn to say no. You must learn to stand up and face any person trying to completely dominate your life or to take over your life. Some ways to stop mind control include:

Stop mind games: If you realize that a person is playing mind games with your life, you need to stop them. Mind games such as guilt-tripping, projecting, playing hard to get, etc. may give a person full access to your min. Since you know that such games are dangerous, you must stop them before they go far. Do not allow a person to penetrate your mind and play games with your feelings. If you spot such games, just stand up and face the person and tell them to get out of your life or to stop the games.

Learn emotional control: Mind control starts with emotional control. A person only plays mind games if they know that they will affect your emotions. In cases such as testing your limits, a person may use mind games that try to provoke your emotional reaction. If such a person realizes that you cannot be provoked emotionally, he/she will be frustrated and leave you alone. Just by being able to hide your emotions, you can put off a lot of people who try to control your mind. Manipulative people will only stay around and try controlling your mind if they see their tactics working. If a controlling person realizes that their tactics can get to your mind, they will keep on using them. You must learn to hide your emotions if you wish to put off such individuals from your life.

Face the manipulator: If a person is trying to control your mind, the chances are that they are afraid of you or they do not want you to have power. In this case, it is much easier for you to stop such people by confronting them. Just by letting them know that you are aware of their tactics, you completely shut them down. Mind controlling individuals like to think of themselves as being wise than everybody else. However, if you can read their intentions and let them know that you are aware of their manipulative intentions, you will completely stop them from taking manipulative actions. It takes a lot of courage to confront manipulative persons face to face. However, this is one way you can be sure that you protect yourself from manipulation.

Stopping mind control requires that you pay keen attention to the control tactics used. You need to master all the common manipulation and control tactics. Once you know the tactics, it is easy for you to spot them as soon as they start. If you are keen enough, you will be able to spot control during the very early stages of the relationship. For instance, if you know how love-bombing works, you will not allow any stranger to come to your life with love bombing tactics.

What Is Hypnosis

Hypnosis is a psychological technique that involves the induction of a state of consciousness in which the practitioner loses the power of voluntary action. When a person is in a hypnotic state, they lose touch with the physical world and only focus or operate in the new world. In hypnosis, a new world/environment is created in the mind of the practitioner through visualization. A person can be heard talking to other people in the other world. When a person is in a hypnotic state, he/she is highly responsive to suggestions or directions. Hypnosis is used in therapy to help people who suffer from various ailments recover.

Although hypnosis is a practice that has been around for quite some time, it is still among the very controversial therapeutic techniques. While some psychologists suggest that a person in a hypnotic state has no control over their actions, others argue that a person cannot completely lose their free will.

Generally, hypnosis can happen naturally or can be induced. Natural hypnosis happens without the practitioner knowing or asking for it. Psychologists believe that an adult human being has to go through a hypnotic state at least once per day. We will be looking at some examples of the hypnotic states later. With that said, a hypnotic state that occurs naturally cannot be used to control your mind and actions. The hypnotic state that is induced works well when it comes to controlling your mind.

One of the ways of getting a person into the hypnotic state is by using music. If you play music that plays at the rate of 45 to 72 bits per minute, you are likely to transform the mind of a person into the hypnotic state. The message within such music can be used to transform the thinking and the ideas of a person. This is because the music plays at the same rate as your heartbeat. As a result, every beat of the song is perfectly synchronized with your mind.

The other option for induced hypnosis includes guided hypnosis. Guided hypnosis is the most common type of hypnosis, which occurs at a therapist's table. Hypnosis can only be performed by a hypnotist. Hypnotists take the victim through a visual journey that can be used to transform the thinking of a person.

Hypnosis uses guided relaxation and intense concentration to achieve a heightened state of awareness(trance). In this state of mind, the person's attention is heightened to such an extent that he may not experience or recognize anything that is going around. You have probably seen a person crossing the road with their mind focused on their phone to such an extent that they are almost hit by a car. This is a person in a natural state of hypnosis. When you are in a hypnotic state, you do not feel or experience the world around you. Everything is focused on the new world that you have created within your mind. You must allow yourself to come back to the real world to start experiencing a normal life again. Hypnosis is characterized by two factors:

- **Suggestion therapy:** Through suggestive therapy, a person is made to respond to suggestions. When a hypnotist performs hypnosis on a person, that person only focuses on the suggestions being given by the hypnotist. Hypnosis has been used to help individuals change their habits, such as stop smoking and nail-biting.

- **Analysis:** An experienced hypnotist can use hypnosis to achieve a different result from the common. For instance, the hypnotist can take the practitioner through a relaxed state of events just to extract important information. The analysis process helps the therapist determine the root cause of mental or social disorders.

Why Do People Use Hypnosis?

Although manipulative people use hypnosis for mind control, the use of hypnosis in psychology is very different. Hypnosis was invented as a method of treating people for various conditions. Hypnosis is used in the treatment of the following conditions:

- **Phobias and fears:** Through guided hypnosis, a person suffering from phobia or fear can be helped to change their mind. People who suffer from fear are only in such a situation because of past life experiences. The human brain works in connection with emotional experiences. When a person undergoes a negative emotional experience, the mind records the instance and stores it in the subconscious. If the negative instance was painful, a person develops fear for similar experiences. The emotional association of experiences to certain emotions can make a person fearful even when there is no threat in the vicinity. For this reason, a guided hypnosis process is needed to change a person's emotional association of circumstances. For instance, if a person associated darkness with danger, a hypnotist may use guided suggestions to take the practitioner into darkness and show them that darkness can be safe. Matter of fact, through guided hypnosis, you can completely change the perception of a person about a certain subject. Instead of experiencing fear, you can make the practitioner start experiencing love. A hypnotist can take the practitioner into the darkness just to introduce them to a person they love so much.

- **Sleep disorders**: Sleep disorders often lead to a lack of sleep at night or oversleeping during the day. Such disorders can affect your functioning during the day. A person experiences fatigue and tiredness if they lack sufficient sleep at night. If you have been experiencing difficulty to sleep, you need to deal with all the sleep disorders. Some sleep disorders can be handled by undergoing a hypnosis session. One of the ways to get to sleep when you are being disturbed by thoughts in the middle of the night is counting sheep. Through a simple meditation process, visualize yourself in a farm and start counting sheep. This process works because the human mind cannot focus on other things when counting numbers. If you close your eyes and get yourself to another world, where you count sheep, you will easily get to seep. Hypnosis can be used to help you sleep in many other ways. If you suffer from insomnia, you can also have a person guide you into a state of hypnosis. The hypnotist must take you to a safe world for you to experience sleep easily.

- **Depression:** Hypnosis can also be used in treating depression and anxiety. A person only gets depressed or anxious due to worries of the future. When you are in a hypnotic state, you are in an entirely new world where you have to let go of all your worries. Hypnosis is used to relieve the pressure on your mind due to overthinking. When you allow your mind to get into a place where you feel safe and welcomed, you no longer have to focus on your problems. Your mind and body are in a relaxed state simply because you are not in touch with your real-life problems. For a moment, you let go of all your problems and just focus on a beautiful world that is created by the hypnotist.

- **Post-trauma anxiety:** Hypnosis has also been found to be helpful to individuals who suffer PDST and other types of post-traumatic anxiety. After going through a traumatic experience, a person may be unable to concentrate. Images of past traumatic events may send a person into a state of anxiety and constant worry. The use of hypnosis helps change the emotional association of traumatic memory triggers. For instance, after going through a traumatic moment in the hands of policemen, a person may consider all police persons dangerous. If such a person spots a police person, they may experience panic attacks and anxiety. However, through guided suggestions, the person may be helped to start associating police persons with security and not a risk as it is the case. It is difficult for many people who have suffered traumatic events to heal, especially when they have to live with traumatic memory triggers daily. The use of hypnosis is vital in helping such patients change their emotional association to certain events. This is the only sure way to get rid of traumatic anxiety.

- Grief and Loss: Hypnosis can also be used to help individuals who are undergoing grief or loss. During painful and emotional moments such as death, it is sometimes impossible to console and comfort a person. The use of hypnosis may work to some extent in making a person relax. You can use hypnosis to calm a person down and make them realize that they are loved and appreciated. Through hypnosis, you can make the victim forget about the painful moment for a few hours and get some time to rest. It is common for people to lack sleep or overthink during such moments. Using hypnosis can help such individuals relax and reduce their thoughts about occurrences.

Examples of Hypnosis and Deception

As mentioned, hypnosis can either occur naturally or can be induced. Manipulative people use induced hypnosis to control a person. When a manipulator wants to use hypnosis, they must first create a good rapport with the victim. In most cases, you cannot perform a hypnotic exercise on a person who is not willing. You must first make the practitioner feel comfortable. Once the practitioner feels comfortable, you build a story that starts from the most basic levels of life. The hypnosis takes the practitioner through a journey of visions until the practitioner gets completely lost in the hypnotic world. When this happens, the hypnotist has the power to start telling the practitioner ideas that are contrary to their beliefs. Most manipulators use their ideologies to brainwash the victims. The hypnotist changes a person's perception of life completely by introducing foreign ideas. Some examples of hypnosis in real life include:

Example 1: Natural daily hypnosis
Every person undergoes natural hypnosis on a daily basis. You have probably been through a moment when your thoughts were lost in another world. When a person is daydreaming or completely lost in their thoughts, they are in a hypnotic state. In this state of mind, you do not perceive your environment. The good news is that when you

are in a state of natural hypnosis, you cannot have another person controlling your mind. In a natural state of hypnosis, you are still in control, and you are responsible for your actions. Although you may not perceive your environment, a person touching you may bring you back to the real world. The only situation where a person is completely out of touch is when hypnosis is induced by another person.

Example 2: Actors and Athletes
 If you wish to perform as an actor or an athlete, you have to allow your mind to be 100% engaged in your action. Many athletes have reported completely losing the focus on the environment and only focusing on their target. If you want to perform as an athlete, you must focus your attention on the goal ahead. You must be the only person in the crowd who does not hear the voice of the people cheering. The same case applies to actors. In many cases, for an actor to perform a scene, they must place everything else at the back of their mind and focus only on the scene. Such a heightened state of attention can make a person perform better in the scene.

How To Deal With Hypnosis
 While being in a hypnotic state is a good thing for performers and athletes, it is also very dangerous. When you are under guided hypnosis or music-induced hypnosis, you are 25% more suggestible. In other words, you easily accept other people's suggestions, and you may take actions that are against your will. For this reason, you must be careful when you allow any person to perform hypnosis on you. Matter of fact, you must never allow any person to lead you into hypnosis unless it is a trusted professional therapist. If you realize that someone is trying hard to get your mind into a hypnotic state, cut communication, and avoid such a person entirely. If you allow people to make such movements next to you, it is easy to get trapped in the world of hypnosis against your will.

Chapter 5: The Dark Triad

Dark psychology is a game that is well orchestrated by the dark triad group. Although all human beings have a dark side, there is a small group of people who tend to show extreme cases of darkness. Such people are characterized by certain social and mental disorders. There are people who are generally socially out of place. They lack a sense of touch with social norms and tend to show exaggerated levels of evil.

If you want to escape dark psychology, you must learn to spot such individuals. You should be in a position to spot any person who shows characteristics of social disorders and run away from them or stop any relationship before it advances to deeper levels.

Understanding Mental Disorders

A person who suffers from mental disorders has a different way of thinking or perception of reality. There are over 300 different mental disorders listed by the DSM(Diagnostic and Statistical Manual of Mental Disorders). These mental disorders vary in range and action. Although there are plenty of mental disorders, only a few are extreme and can be seen outwardly.

When a person is suffering from a certain mental disorder, it is difficult for them to socialize or relate to other people. Mental disorders tend to make people selfish or extremely selfless. Certain mental disorders make people lose self-confidence, while others lead to overconfidence. It is common for people who suffer from mental disorders to be manipulative. It is also common for people who suffer from low self-esteem to try and use manipulation and blackmail to gain public recognition. The same case applies to people who suffer from high self-esteem. They may try to show that they are better by trying to gain control. Mental disorders take a person's dark side to the extreme. Some individuals who suffer from mental disorders completely dissociate with human feelings. Lack of emotions in such individuals may lead to violence, and as a result, such individuals perform painful abusive acts without fear. It is important for you to understand all the forms of mental disorders and be on the watch out for dangerous mental disorders.

The Top 7 Mental Disorders

- **Mood disorders:** Mood disorders refer to a mental state where a person may experience episodes of a bad mood all over sudden. Although all people experience bad moods once in a while, a person suffering from mood disorders experiences extreme negativity during such disorders. When the bad mood occurs, the patient may get violent and abusive. Such people only try using mind control and manipulation when they are experiencing a bad mood episode. Although the bad moods do not last for many days, a person can do a lot of harm within the short hours of a bad mood. Some of the common conditions that are categorized under mood disorders include depression and bipolar disorders among others.

- **Personality disorders:** Personality disorders refer to a situation where a person has a different personality compared to other people. Most people suffering from personality disorders have a different perception of social life. They do not easily socialize with other people and have a different way of perceiving human emotions. People who suffer from personality disorders are likely to cause harm and manipulation. Examples of personality disorders include narcissistic personality disorder and borderline personality disorder.

- **Psychotic disorders:** Psychotic personality disorder refers to individuals who have a psychological or mental difference from others. In this case, the patient's thinking is limited or insufficient. Such people may be seen to be normal, but a keen observation shows that they are short in some way. Although they may not be termed to be out of their minds, they are not 100 percent sober. People who suffer from a psychotic personality disorder may be found talking to themselves or lost in their thoughts. Such individuals may also use mind control and manipulation to gain whatever they want. An example of conditions in psychotic disorders includes schizophrenia patients.

- **Eating disorders:** Eating disorder applies to people who experience abnormal eating habits. In most cases, eating disorders are brought about by habitual eating or emotional disorders. A person may overeat when they are undergoing a tough emotional situation while others only overeat because they are used to eating too much. Eating disorders do not affect a person to the extent of manipulation. However, a person who suffers from eating disorders may use underhand tactics where food is involved. If you live with such a person, you may be forced to cater to their excessive appetite, or otherwise, you may end up starving.

- **Trauma-related disorders**: Traumatic disorders refer to a situation where a person behaves or acts differently due to traumatic life experiences. A person who has undergone traumatic life experiences has a more fragile personality. Their emotions are easily triggered, and such people may experience anxiety and depression. The people who have undergone traumatic events in life try had to avoid going through a similar occasion. In their quest to self-protect, they end up hurting the people who are close to them. Traumatic disorder patients are likely to use manipulation and dark psychology tactics just to protect themselves from undergoing similar traumatic occurrences. Some of the common traumatic disorders include Post Traumatic Stress Disorder PTSD, Narcissistic abuse syndrome, and substance abuse disorder. Such individuals are only dark and manipulative because they want to protect themselves from a harmful world. Their actions of self-protection are may end up being harmful, but their ultimate intentions do not include hurting any person.

Narcissism

Narcissism is a personality disorder in which the patient has an inflated sense of self-worth. A narcissistic person considers themselves worthier and more superior than all the people around them. This s grandiose sense of self-worth leads narcissistic individuals into performing acts that include humiliation and disregard for other people. A narcissistic person may hurt and humiliate others just to get recognition. Narcissists are known to demand attention from the people around them and always strive to show that they are right. People who suffer from narcissistic personality disorder are very dangerous and can be very manipulative.

Narcissism is the heart of all dark psychology tactics. Any person suffering from narcissism will use blackmail, brainwashing, hypnosis, persuasion, and any other means possible to gain control. Narcissists strive to be in control of relationships for personal gain and glorification. When a narcissistic person starts a relationship, the main aim is to have power and control over the people that they are controlling.

People who suffer from narcissistic personality disorder also have fragile self-esteem. The slightest criticism can lead to aggression. Although such individuals outwardly show high self-esteem, psychologists believe that they use an outward ego to hide internal insecurities. If a person suffers from a narcissistic personality disorder, they strive hard to be seen as perfect beings in the eyes of the public. If you wish to protect yourself from dark psychologists, then you must protect yourself from narcissists. Here are some characteristics of narcissistic individuals that will help you spot them from a distance.

Characteristics of Narcissists

Have an exaggerated sense of self-importance: A narcissistic person thinks that he/she is important than everybody else. For this reason, they will expect special treatment and even demand special treatment. They are easily angered if they do not receive any specialized treatment.

Have a sense of entitlement: People who suffer from narcissistic personality disorder think that they are entitled to own whatever they want. Their sense of entitlement is extended to human beings, and they often view people as personal property. When narcissists want to be in a relationship with another person, they will try to make the relationship work even if the other person is not interested. Narcissists believe that they should get whatever they want without being questioned or challenged.

Expect to be recognized as superior: Narcissists do not expect to be treated equally or to be looked at as equal to other people. Even if they do not have any achievement that warrants a status of superiority, narcissists will demand to be treated and looked at as being superior.

Exaggerate achievements and talents: Narcissistic persons think that they are more talented and better than other people. They deem their abilities and talents special as compared to what other people can do. Even when they are working in a group, they deem their talents and contribution more important than anyone else's.

Be preoccupied with fantasies about success and power: Narcissistic individuals do not accept their status of life. They are constantly talking about success and power as if they belong to a different social class. Narcissistic individuals only associate with people who seem to belong to their social class. They are always preoccupied with talk about money, power, and control.

Monopolize conversation: Narcissists try to show their power and superiority by controlling conversations. They do not allow other people to have an equal opportunity to air out their opinion on a certain matter. When they allow other people to speak out, they end up belittling their ideas. A narcissistic person will belittle any person who tries to challenge their authority. Since they perceive most people as being inferior, they do not pay attention to any person they deem inferior.

Expect special favors and unquestioning: Narcissistic persons do not expect to be treated in the same way as the world treats others. For this reason, a narcissistic person expects to be asked questions that are favorable. Since narcissists are people who see themselves as superior, they expect the respect to be accorded to them whenever they are asked any questions.

Take advantage of others to get what they want: Narcissistic individuals do not hesitate to take advantage of others. For a narcissist, the end justifies the means. They can hurt a person or even kill as long as they get whatever they want. Narcissists are very manipulative and are known to brainwash their victims before obtaining whatever they want from the relationship.

Have an inability or unwillingness to recognize the needs and feelings of others: Narcissistic individuals only think about personal needs. The reason why narcissists are very dangerous is that they can hurt a person without thinking about it twice. They will do anything necessary without perceiving the feelings of others. Narcissists are known to impact chronic pain and torture to victims without thinking about the feelings of their victims.

Envious of others and believe others envy them: Narcissistic individuals show envy to any person who has achieved more or tries to achieve more. For this reason, narcissistic individuals use sabotage to stop others from achieving more. If you are in a relationship with a narcissistic person, you may realize that he/she is trying to block all your attempts at success, either socially or academically. They will strive hard to block your ways and ensure that you remain at the same level or even go lower than you used to be.

Behave arrogantly or haughtily: Most narcissistic persons do not show humility or patience when they are among others. They are boastful and naughty and are often seen as being boastful. They believe that whatever they own is better than the things that other people own.

Machiavellianism

Machiavellianism is a personality disorder in which a person only focuses on personal needs and interests. A person who suffers from Machiavellianism may use manipulation and deceptive tactics to gain whatever they want in life. This type of personality is one of the dark personalities and can be very dangerous. A person who suffers from Machiavellianism is only interested in getting whatever they want, no matter the means used to get it.

Characteristics Of Machiavellianism

Only focused on their ambition and interests: Machiavellianism leads a person to focus on personal interests and have less regard for the interests of others. Such people do not pay attention to the feelings or desires of the people around them.

Prioritize money and power over relationships: People who suffer from Machiavellianism do not deem relationships important in any way. They can break up any relationship as long as they gain money and power. Such individuals only get into a relationship to gain money or power.

Come across as charming and confident: Like all manipulative persons, individuals who suffer from Machiavellianism come across as very charming and confident in the early stages of the relationship. They are known to use love bombing to attract people to themselves. Once they attract you into the trap, they will use you to get whatever they want before dumping you and moving on to the next victim.

Exploit and manipulate others to get ahead: They are usually successful based on the hard work of others. Such individuals do not hesitate to manipulate a person. They will work hard to ensure that they collect wealth and resources from every person they relate to. As a result, they gain money and wealth from manipulating others.

Lie and deceive when required: Machiavellianism is characterized by lies and deception at the highest levels. For such individuals to gain control and manipulate a person into giving out money, they must lie. They lie about everything, including their names and personal life. A person who practices Machiavellianism may have multiple names and use all of them to gain wealth.

Lacking in principles and values: Such individuals do not attach much value to life. They often live a useless life and do not spend their money responsibly. In most cases, they lack a stable family or lasting friendships. They only live by collecting money and wealth from people when it is convenient

Capable of causing others to achieve their means: Those who practice Machiavellianism can achieve anything without getting involved in the dirty work. Since they use manipulation tactics to get control, they are willing to do anything possible as long as they achieve their desired result. Most people who practice Machiavellianism like to keep their names clean when handling dirty deals.

 Low levels of empathy: Just like narcissists, those who practice Machiavellianism do not have feelings or emotional attachment to people. They can hurt others without feeling remorse or showing concern. They are okay as long as they achieve their main goal. The only thing that matters to such people is wealth and power. As long as they have power and control, they are happy to be doing whatever they are doing.

 Often avoid commitment and emotional attachments: Because they only get into relationships for personal gain, most people who practice Machiavellianism avoid commitments. They try as much as possible to remain out of the relationship circle. When they date a person, they do not commit to marriage; instead, they simply stay in relationships as a trial and error system.

Psychopathy

A psychopath is a person who suffers from a psychopathic personality disorder. This refers to a personality that is characterized by a complete lack of empathy or social relation. A person who suffers from psychopathic personality disorder is likely to use manipulation to achieve whatever they want in life.
Psychopathy is one of the difficult personality disorders to spot because it does not have obvious signs, as we have seen in narcissism or Machiavellianism. A psychopathic person tries as much as possible to be seen as normal. The main reason why psychopathic individuals remain unknown is that they do not socialize as much as other people. Individuals who suffer from psychopathic personality disorder stand out as discrete persons who maintain a low profile.

Psychopathic individuals often end up doing shocking acts due to their lack of conscience. A person who suffers from a psychopathic personality disorder can commit murder right in public and walk away as if nothing happened. Their personality is among the most complex and the least understood by psychologists. Most psychologists try placing a finger on the actions and the reasons behind the actions of psychopaths without success.

Psychopaths and sociopaths share the same characteristics, and the two words are often used interchangeably. However, there is a slight difference between the two personalities. A psychopath may commit serious acts of extreme torture even leading to murder without any reason. On the other hand, sociopaths often have a motive of gaining money and wealth.

Chapter6: How to Read and Analyze People

Now that you know the different types of dark personalities that are out there to control your life, you need to stop them before they touch your life. The best way of escaping dark psychologists is being able to spot them and run away in advance. You should be in a position to determine the behavior and actions of a person and run away from a dark person before they gain access to your life. If you allow a dark person into your life, it becomes impossible for you to move out of the relationship.

How to Read People

Given that you are trying to understand the character of every person you interact with, it is important that you learn to read people. Once you are in a position to read a person, you can separate the good people from the evil ones. In this section, we will be looking at the available techniques of reading people. First, there are the general techniques you will be needing in order to read people:

Create a baseline: You cannot understand any person if you do not have a point of reference. If you want to spot a person who has a personality or mental disorder, you should have a baseline. Although people behave differently, there should be basic factors that sound an alarm when you meet a new person. Setting a baseline entails putting in place measures or factors of consideration that will determine your interactions. When you set a baseline, there are factors that you put in place to protect yourself from extreme personalities. You may decide that you will not allow any person in your life if they try controlling your actions. You may also decide to avoid all people who are too sweet at the start. You may choose to set a very specific detailed baseline or a general one. In either case, you can use such a baseline to observe the characters of people. In your basic expectation, you need to see a person who behaves in a certain way and decide whether to let them in your life or not.

Look for deviations: After setting a baseline, look for all deviations from the baseline. For instance, you know that when you meet a new person, you will first greet and exchange a few pleasantries. A deviation would be a case where you are meeting a person for the first time, and they want to hug you so tightly as if you have known each other for ages. When you have a baseline, you understand how humans behave in certain situations. You are open to observing any behaviors that are outside the norm. When you are meeting a new person, you can easily observe how they talk about themselves and spot a person who is self-absorbed.

Notice clusters of gestures: Clusters of gestures include activities or actions that a person does over and over. When you are meeting a new person, you expect that they are unique in a certain way. For you to spot their uniqueness, you have to observe their actions. A person who is unique in a certain way may do certain actions over and over again. When you have a person who does something specific repeatedly, or they do a certain action in a specific way, you should be able to note it down. Noting down clusters of gestures will help you draw clues about a person and their personality.

Compare and contrast: The other way of understanding a person's personality is comparison. If you are meeting someone, you may choose to compare their actions to another person. If you know a person who suffers from a certain mental disorder, you can try comparing their actions. This is especially important if you feel that something is off. If you look at a person and realize that they do not act in a normal way, you may try comparing their actions to other people. A comparison will let you know if a person is slightly off the radar.

Look into the mirror: Looking into the mirror simply means comparing a person's actions to your own. Ask yourself, what would I do if I was in the same position? For instance, if you are meeting a new person in your life and they keep on talking about something specific, you could examine yourself and try to gauge your actions if you were in their shoe. If you deem yourself as a normal person, the actions of the people you meet should not be very far off. A person should not act as if they are new to this world. If you come across a person who seems too new to your world, you have to give them special attention. Try finding out why a certain person is behaving in a specific way.

Identify the strong voice: Every time you interact with a new person, there will be a voice from within that will speak to you about their personality. Pay attention to your sixth sense and try observing the personality of the person you are meeting.

Body Language

Body language is an important aspect that can help us analyze people. The actions that a person takes when you are having a conversation speak a lot. If you are a keen person, you may be able to draw a lot of information from a person's body language. NLP experts rely on body language to extract important data. The information can be obtained through the posture, position of arms, and other aspects of the body during communication. Some of the important aspects of body language to consider in a conversation include:

Pay attention to the position of the arms: People wrap arms around their chest and lean back to show authority. In a seating position, a person may cross their legs and spread their arms around a chair to show superiority. It is important to read such signs. If you do not know how to interpret the meaning of gestures such as the position of the arms, the movement of the arms, among others, you may never be able to influence people. You must look at the position of a person's arms and be able to tell if a person wants attention. People use the positions of the arm to demand respect.

Observe the eyes: It is difficult for most people to maintain eye contact when they are speaking lies. If you wish to understand a person you are talking to more, you must pay attention to their eye movements. A person is paying the most attention when their eyes are focused on you. Do not keep on talking to a person who is paying attention to their phone or is busy on their computer. You should aim at having the full attention of the audience to ensure that the message arrives home.

Pay attention to proximity: The distance between you and the person you are talking to determines the level of relationship and the type of conversation. In a professional conversation, there must be a safe distance between the two individuals. There is less contact, and every word is explained to clarity. However, in a personal conversation, people talk when they are much closer to each other. The privacy levels of a discussion also determine the proximity.

Watch the head movements: The head plays an important role in body language. Nodding of the head is the traditional sign of approval. Some people will not talk much but will keep on nodding their heads during a conversation. It is your duty to ensure that the person you are talking to is listening. One of the ways to gauge their attention is by looking at their heads. However, it is not a must that a person nods their head if they are paying attention. Some people just listen without having to nod.

Pay attention to the legs and standing posture: The feet and the standing posture play an important role in interpreting the attention of a person. You can tell if a person is paying attention just by looking at their feet. You can also tell if a person is comfortable with the conversation. If a person feels uncomfortable, they will keep on moving their feet anxiously. A person may look composes on the eye, but the feet may tell a different story. You should be observant of all these factors to tell if someone is paying attention. When a person is listening and comfortable with the conversation, their feet will be firm on the ground with minimum movements. This only applies when you are standing during the conversation. If the conversation happens in a place where all the parties are seated the situation might be slightly different. However, in either case, it is important to pay attention to the legs. Pay attention to the movement of legs, toes, and the overall standing posture. It will help you understand what a person thinks and what the person wants in life

Look out for hand signals: Hands can also be used to pass around a lot of information. For instance, if someone is frustrated, they may throw their hands in the air. This is a show of arrogance or frustration. You must be able to read and interpret hand signals. There are some points that cannot be explained by words alone. In such cases, people use hands to try and explain the point. Hands are commonly used to clarify points. If you are trying to pass around some information and it turns out that you are short of vocabulary, you may use your hands. If you wish to be a good manipulator, you must learn to pay attention to hands and know how to read hand signals.

Human Behavior

Human behavior may also help you understand a person and note down their personality. The best way to study people is to observe daily actions. In some instances, you may even provoke a person just to see their actions. Human behavior best comes out during emotional moments and frustration. If you want to understand a person in detail, you must pay attention to their actions when they are in a bad mood. You must also learn to pay attention to people when no one else is watching. Some people even use spy cameras just to capture a person's behavior when no one else is watching. If you want to read a person, there are specific aspects of human behavior that you need to pay attention to. Some of the aspects of human behavior that will help you understand a person's personality include

Emotional reaction: Emotional reaction is the one important aspect of human behavior that can help you learn more about a person. The expressive aspect of a person's emotions will tell you whether a person has a normal personality, or they suffer from a personality disorder. Individuals who suffer from personality disorders show a different reaction to emotional situations. When they are provoked, they may be very aggressive and reactive. Although people are supposed to react to emotional provocation, you should avoid any person who reacts to the extreme. At the same time, you must be very careful with people who show no reaction at all. Individuals who are manipulative tend to bypass all the emotional moments as if nothing is happening. If you realize that a certain person does not show any reaction to emotional moments, step back and try understanding them better.

Silent time: Another important aspect of human behavior that you must observe is actions taken during silent times. There are people who show their true characters when they are silent or alone. You may realize that a person gets nervous or worried during silent moments. Observing such characters will help you understand a person and get to know their personality.

Daily routine: Another option when it comes to observing human behavior is paying attention to a daily routine. Routine simply includes the activities that a person takes daily. Every organized person has a routine for their life. A person only shows how organized and stable they are through their routine. An organized person will have a clear flow of events starting with the sleep time up to the time they wake up.

Certain Words

Words are also a vital part of a conversation. When it comes to the meaning of words, you have to look past what a person says. As we have noted, only 7 percent of a conversation is carried through words. However, through NLP techniques, you can extract more than 50% of a conversation from words. This means that there is a special way of paying attention to words. Do not just take what people say for what it is. The most important information is not what a person says when they are describing themselves. For instance, if you ask a person to introduce themselves, do not just accept the information they give you. It is during such conversations where words only account for 7% of the truth. In reality, you should try to understand a person's conversation by paying serious attention to words during different discussions. Some of the factors to consider when analyzing a person's words include:

Word patterns: When a person talks, they will use a certain pattern of words or sentence structure. If you are keen enough, you will realize that the same pattern reflects in their writing. The pattern of words depends on a person's wiring. If a person is wired to focus on visualization, they are likely to use a visualization approach to life. They will use words such as imagine, observe, think about, etc. The sentence structure of such a person is biased in a visualization structure to make a person have a vivid view of the subject of communication. If you want to influence such a person, you must also use a visual approach. If a person uses an audio approach in their conversations, you should also try using an audio approach when targeting their minds.

Repeated words: Repeated words are ones that a person uses more often. If a person keeps on using certain words, the chances are that they are that those words form the anchor of their beliefs. For instance, a person who is religious may not speak for long without mentioning God. Their entire belief system is built around the supernatural. As so, the individual will spend a lot of time talking about the supernatural.

Cursing words: Cursing words are also an integral part that will make you understand the person you are talking to. Cursing words can also show the integral belief systems of a person. The person will curse using words that constantly go through their minds. If you can detect and try to fish out information from words that a person uses when they are frustrated, such as the cursing words, you may be in a position to learn a lot about a specific person.

Intonation and stress: The other factor that can help you observe a person or study their character is the intonation used in words. For instance, a person may use stress on words that carry more weight in a conversation. Through paying attention to the tone of a person, you can detect the emotional orientation and the value a person attaches to certain words. When a person is in an emotional state, it is common to hear their voice getting sharp or raised. Such factors can help you understand the emotional state of a person. If you pay attention to intonation, you will be able to notice when a person is in a bad emotional condition. You can also detect when a person is feeling good or when they are happy.

Be Specific

The other aspect that will help you study people is specification. If you want to understand the operations or the thinking of a person, you can try being specific in certain areas. You can try asking straight forward questions that will not give the person a chance to hide behind the bushes. A specific person will directly point out something wrong as being bad or something as good as being good. When you choose to approach a person based on specifics, your aim is to ensure that you get the details of a conversation or the action you are doing.

Specification in conversations: Being specific in a conversation is one way you can gauge whether a person is being genuine or false. If a person is lying, you can realize it from their eyes or their actions. When you target a specific person, or you try to fish out specific information, a person will tell you the truth. Even if they try lying, you will be in a position to spot the lies. You must be willing to ask direct questions if you want to get direct information from a person. However, do not try using the specific question approach unless you have built a good relationship with the person you are talking to.

Chapter 7: Understanding Your Identity

When it comes to dealing with the darkness in the world, you must realize that you are also part of the problem. As much as there are many dark people in the world, you are not so good yourself. There are many actions that you do that display your dark side. If you wish to be a person who stays from the dark life, you need to address the dark side in your mind.

The first question you must answer when trying to address dark psychology is, "Who are you?" Do you relate to the dark side or are you on the light side? Although most people like to think of themselves as being on the right side of life, it is clear that darkness takes root in many people. The dark side of life cannot be completely avoided. As you focus on your personality and your thoughts, you may realize that you have some dark desires that lay in wait. The extent to which you execute your dark desires or the level at which you solve all the problems associated with darkness determines your ability to stand against it.

Through your thoughts and your ideas, you can also detect the darkness in other people. If you manage to control the voices inside your head, you will be in a position to control darkness and how it manifests around you. However, you must first find your identity. One of the best ways to find your identity is through meditation. Meditation helps you realize the different aspects of your environment that you did not pay attention to. If you wish to realize your identity and know who you are and how you operate, you should sharpen the following skills.

Self-awareness: Self-awareness is the ability to detect and monitor your actions and emotions. In everyday life, you make choices that are informed by your emotions. Although few people pay attention to their emotions, it is a fact that emotions play an integral part in deciding who you are and whatever you do. The actions you take on a daily basis determine your personality.

However, these actions are, most importantly determined by your emotions. You should be able to pay attention to your emotions and how they affect your actions. A person who is emotionally aware is sensitive to all the actions they take. If you are self-aware, you strive hard to ensure that you do not give emotions room to control your life. Emotional awareness is the power that helps you know your strengths and weaknesses in every situation you go through. When you are undergoing a tough emotional situation, you can gauge your limits. You get to know how dark you are and how impulsive you get. Most people get emotional and impulsive during difficult emotional moments. It is necessary to observe your actions when you are under pressure so that you may be able to tell if you get out of control during emotions.

Mindfulness: Mindfulness is a form of meditation that allows you to focus on yourself. This is one of the best ways to try and know your identity. In mindfulness, the practitioner focuses on their thoughts, body, or emotions. A person practicing mindfulness must focus on the emotions or thoughts that go through their mind at the time of meditation. Mindfulness is one of the most responsive ways of meditation. Mindfulness will help you know the deepest secrets that have been hiding in your subconscious mind. When you practice mindfulness, you will realize that you have some dark desires that you have never thought existed. It is important to keep it in your mind that such desires may cause you to have doubts about yourself. For this reason, mindfulness meditation is practiced under certain rules.

Rules of Mindfulness Meditation

No judgment: The first and the most important rule of mindful meditation is that the practitioner must be non-judgmental. When you focus your mind and thoughts on your personality, you will realize that you also have a dark side. The dark desires that stay within a person are usually hidden in public behavior. However, a careful examination of yourself may reveal some dirty thoughts. It is important to ensure that you stick to observing yourself without being judgmental in any way. Even if you realize that you have a dark personality, you should allow yourself to enjoy your personality in the moment of meditation without raising any questions to yourself.

No regret: Another important aspect of meditation is that you do not regret any actions or thoughts you make. If you practice mindfulness, everything you experience and observe about yourself should remain in the world in which you were observing. If you observe anything positive, you should be happy for yourself, but the positive moment must be left within the mindfulness room. The same case applies to all the negative aspects you may observe about yourself. There is no doubt about the fact that there are many dark sides to a person. All the dark parts you observe about your feelings and desires should not be a cause for judgment. You must allow yourself to observe negativity without being regretful in any way. Even if you visualize yourself doing something dirty you must not regret it.

Acceptance: Acceptance is another aspect of meditation that must be used if you want to enjoy the practice. The fact that you will be focusing on a detailed observation of your body and thoughts means that there are many things you may not like about yourself. You need to learn to accept the situation and move on. For instance, if you realize that you do not like the shape of your body or the look of your face, you still have to accept and move on with life. You must never dwell on the outcome of mindful meditation in any negative way. If possible, you should only take the positives from such a practice.

Communication: The other aspect that will help you understand your identity is communication. Just the same way you pay attention to the communication of others, you must also pay attention to your communication. If you observe your communication, you will realize that there are many factors that make you different. By observing your verbal and non-verbal communication, you can draw important information from your language. You will be able to identify your dark side and determine your social aspects. All the dark personalities we have addressed above can easily be identified by observing communication means. The same case applies at a personal level. Although most people tend to be selfish and biased when observing their actions, it is important that you allow yourself the chance to look at your communications in a sober way. Try observing your arguments and gauge your dominance in a conversation. If you realize that you always try to dominate conversations or you must always win an argument, pay close attention to your personality. You need to start watching your dark side because you have one.

The Voice Inside Our Head and How We Can Overcome It for the Better

One of the reasons why people practice dark psychology is that they listen to a voice of selfish desires. The voice within your head keeps on encouraging you to go out and do something for yourself. You will find that most people listen to the dark voice that pushes them to achieve personal desires. It is important for you to learn to silence the negative voice that speaks to you. This voice is only interested in personal welfare and does not care for the emotions of others.

If you realize that the negative voice in your mind always gains control over your actions, the chances are that you are a dark person. If you can get a genuine opinion from your close friends and family, you will learn that you are manipulative, selfish and to many people arrogant. You need to learn to control all the negative voices that speak to you in all situations. You must train yourself to silence negative voices that may drive you into taking an action that you may regret later. When you realize that you constantly think in a negative way, you must purpose in your mind to take actions that will help you silence the negative voices. Some of the ways to overcome negative voices in your mind include:

Consider other peoples' emotions: The only reason why manipulative people used dark psychology to gain whatever they want is that they do not consider the emotions of others. To start considering the emotions of others, you need to train your imagination. You cannot consider another person unless you can imagine yourself being in the same situation. A person who understands and considers the emotions of others thinks about the people around them. If you have been in a certain situation, it is easy for you to relate to it. However, if you have not been in a similar situation, it becomes difficult for you to consider it. When you train your imagination, you can try to place yourself into the shoe of another person and feel the pain they are going through. Individuals who are empathetic try so much to see that they feel the pain of others. If you are an empathetic person, you try to set yourself in the shoe of other people. You think about the pain they go through and try hard to help in any way possible.

Practice love and kindness meditation: Love and kindness meditation will also help you get rid of all the negative voices in your head. Love and kindness meditation is focused on doing good. When you practice this type of meditation, you visualize yourself as the center of love and kindness in the world. People who practice this type of meditation usually visualize a world where people are craving for love. As the central source of love and kindness, you visualize yourself extending love to all people in the world. This type of meditation is very helpful for people who have suffered abuse. If you have been abused before and the dark voice in your mind is prompting you to try revenge, you need to try this type of mediation.

How to Practice Love and Kindness Meditation

Step1: Find the right spot, where you will enjoy calm and quietness with minimal interruptions. The meditation session should take between 15 minutes and an hour.

Step2: Focus your mind on one person you hate so much and start thinking about them in a good way. When you focus on this person, think of yourself as the center of love. Visualize yourself extending love to this person and all the people in the world who need to be shown, love. As the center of love, visualize yourself walking to a hopeless person, such as a street child, and giving them gifts. Be the person who shows people that life can be beautiful.

Step3: Extend your love to the real-life: As soon as you start realizing the peace associated with extending love to the world, you need to take your practice to the next level. Just meditating and visualizing is not good enough. Walkout and try extending love and kindness to a person who may need it. Buy someone a gift and just try to put a smile on the face of another person. Such gestures will help you start focusing on the positive aspects of life and deal with all the negative aspects of life.

Learn emotional control: The other way of dealing with the negative voice in your mind is learning emotional control. It is a fact that most people only get negative when they are under emotional pain. If someone said something painful to you, the chances are that you may try to revenge. Your desire to revenge and cause pain to another person is brought about by the dark side. To be able to silence all the negative dark voices in your mind, you need to learn to control your emotions. You need to find alternative ways of emotional release. If you realize that painful emotions make you take actions that you do not want, you need to stop them. There are many methods of alternative emotional release. For instance, instead of getting violent when you are angry, you may choose to workout. A simple exercise might help you get all the painful emotions out of your chest. This is one of the ways of dealing with negative voices. Another option is turning negative emotions into positive ones. For instance, if you are feeling angry, you may choose to engage in activities that will make you feel happy. Most people engage in activities such as listening to music, watching comedy shows, or any other activity that may cause a person to smile. It is important for you to ensure that you stay in control of all your actions even when your emotions are on the brink. If you do not know how to control your emotions, people will come in and try controlling your life. You must learn to control your actions and stop the bad thoughts that are associated with all the negativity in your mind.

Learn communication skills: Communication skills will help you learn that; you do not have to be in control always. Communication skills can teach you a lot of factors in regards to controlling yourself and controlling your emotions. If you want to try stopping the negative voices in your mind, first learn to think before speaking. The words that come out of your mouth must be measured. You must pay keen attention to your actions and words in a communication process. The actions you take and your posture also plays an important role in influencing negativity. A person who listens more and speaks less has a chance to filter their thoughts and control the negativity. However, if you speak more and listen less, your mind is controlled by all the negative voices. You may end up speaking anything that may show negativity. You need to learn to control your negative thoughts. You must stop all negative words before they go through your mouth by processing your thoughts accordingly.

Your Inside Voice Knows Dark Psychology Inside Out

Paying attention to the inside voice is the only way to stop dark psychology in your life. You need to realize that the thoughts that go through your mind determine your action. However, there is the possibility of a person controlling their thoughts. You can control your thoughts by:

Interrupting negative thoughts: When you feel that the negative voice is trying to rise in your mind, find something to disrupt your thought process. You may start singing or go out to jog. There are many activities that can help you disrupt your mind from thinking dirty. The more you allow a dirty thought to occupy your mind, the more it takes control. You should learn to say no to any negative voices before they take root in mind.

Positive Behavior: Neuroscientists say that it is possible to change the thoughts of a person by implementing positive activities. If you are a person who has negative habits, the chances are that your thoughts are negative. A person who does not have control over their actions or their daily activities is likely to have dark thoughts. However, if you can change your negative daily actions into positive ones, you may be in a position to completely change how you think. The first step to changing your behavior is developing a daily routine.

If you do not have a positive daily routine, start developing one. Your daily routine should include positive activities that will prompt your mind to think positively. For instance, if you allow one of your daily activities to be visiting orphans, you will soon start developing an emotional bond with orphans. You start realizing the hard life they face on a daily basis. A person who pays attention to orphans or other vulnerable people in society will easily develop empathy. If you pay attention, you start relating to the situations that other people have to face daily. This type of emotional awareness will help you get rid of negative voices in your mind.

Dwelling on the Past

One of the reasons why people allow negative voices to speak to them is past life experiences. A person who has been through a negative life experience may put on a dark face just to protect himself from negativity. A good example is a person who suffers from post-traumatic stress disorder. Such people are manipulative and often see evil in the world. However, their actions are not based on reality. They act based on past traumatic events. If you wish to get rid of any negative voices from your life, you must stop dwelling on the past. People who dwell in the past do not live in the real world. Those who dwell on the past live in a world that is made up of lies and imagination. If you dwell on the past, your life will be characterized by:

Worry: You are always worried, thinking that the activities that happened will happen again. Unfortunately, worry does not bring a solution to any matter. If you find yourself to be worried, try finding a solution to your problem. There is no need thinking so much about a situation that you cannot solve. If you do not have a solution to a problem, then stop thinking about it.

Anxiety: The other problem experienced by those who focus on the past is anxiety and panic attacks. You will find yourself being anxious all the time, thinking about negativity. When you allow the past to control your life, you have to live in constant fear of the unknown. It is important for you to stay aware of such situations and try as much as possible to get rid of worry from your life.

How to Deal with Negative Past

Although you have been through a painful past, you should not allow the pain from the past to dictate the direction of your life. You need to take control and choose to be happy. Letting the negative voices in your mind take control only prolongs your healing process. You must allow yourself a good time to heal from all negative past experiences. People who dwell on the negative past experiences never amount to anything in life. Due to fear, such people are afraid of taking risks or making investments. They are forced to stay at the same level for a very long time, and as a result, they end up living in emotional pain for life. Some of the ways to deal with negative past include:

Acknowledge and Turn it Into Positivity

If you feel that a person or a situation in your past has made it impossible for you to trust people or to trust the world, you must first acknowledge it. Most people live in denial, trying to act as if they have not suffered any type of pain. However, as soon as you choose to accept the situation and agree that you have been hurt, a big weight is lifted off your shoulder. It is important for you to learn the act of accepting situations. There are some situations in life where we cannot do much than accept it. Once you accept that you have been hurt and that you need help with healing, you allow yourself the freedom to move from the painful instance. However, before you acknowledge and allow yourself the time to heal, you will remain in denial, while at the same time, you will continue suffering from the pain caused by that particular instance.

Choose forgiveness: After realizing that you have been hurt by a person, choose to forgive so that you may find healing. If you do not forgive, you may never get healed. It is important to let go of all the pain that you hold in your heart. The first step towards complete healing is forgiveness. When you forgive, you release yourself from the emotional attachment. As a result, you release the pain and remain in peace. Those who choose forgiveness live a much happier and fulfilling life. If you do not forgive, you may never learn to trust again. Trust is an integral part of human relationships. You must accord the people you work with or those you socialize with some form of trust. You should be able to show confidence in people by focusing on their positive aspects. A person who holds on to the pain of past life events does not have room for other people in their life. This is a dangerous situation, given that we need people around us to succeed. As much as you may have wealth, you still need people to enjoy life. You must love and trust and give people the opportunity to be part of your life. This is the beauty of forgiveness that you must seek. If you feel that you have been hurt and that the pain is holding your life back, you must stand up and extend a hand of forgiveness for you to live a happy life once again.

Do Something About It

The only problem with worry and fear is that it does not bring a solution to a problem. You will find that most people, who dwell on the past, allow worry and fear to take root. They are very much afraid of the unknown to such an extent that they cannot make any progress in life. If you chose to focus your mind on the past, you might never enjoy life. Fear and worry will only continue building negative thoughts in your mind. The more you think about the negative experiences from your past, the more you get anxious.

If you are convinced that something negative may happen in your life, the best solution is to do something about it. Instead of dwelling on the past, try doing something that will help prevent any negativity from happening. When you want to live a positive life, you must train yourself to stop overthinking. You must train your mind to focus on the positives of life. Dwelling on the past does not in any way help you move in a positive direction. Dwelling on the past only makes you focus on things that are outdated. You only waste your time thinking about situations that may never reoccur again. Matter of fact, you should be focusing on living a positive life that will stop any negative people from abusing your life.

Chapter 8: Toxic Friendships and Relationships

In this journey of protecting yourself from manipulation, you must realize that manipulation does not come from strangers. The people who manipulate your life are the ones who are closest to your life. Friends and family may come to your life with different intentions. The people you trust the most may turn out to be the manipulative individuals. If you wish to stop manipulative people from controlling your life, you must start by looking at the individuals who are closest to your life.

When it comes to dealing with manipulative friends and family, the situation gets a bit complicated. It is often difficult for most people to spot manipulation in case a close person is involved. This is mainly because people who are close to us blindside our vision with love. When you love a person, you do not imagine that they can do anything to harm your life. In most cases, we are protective even when someone from the outside spots the manipulation. You need to stay sober and think critically about all your relationships. You need to examine the people who are close to you and determine any person who uses manipulation to try and control your life. Spot the signs of manipulation that can come from the people who are close to you.

Signs a Friend or Partner Is Manipulating You

Using your love to gain favors: If a person who is close to you is constantly using your love to gain favors, the chances are that you are under manipulation. Avoid people who use statements such as "if you love me... do you care about me? etc. Such statements are usually used to push a person to do things they did not want to do. If a person asks you to do something for them to prove your love, you are definitely in the wrong relationship. Love does not demand proof. You should not have to do anything to prove that you love a person or you enjoy their company. If you want to stay in peace and enjoy your love with friends and family, they should allow the love to unveil itself naturally,

Playing mind games: If a person who is close to you keeps on playing mind games, the chances are that they are trying to control your life. Mind games include instances such as playing hard to get and taking you on guilt trips. A person may play hard to get just to gain favors from you. It is important for you to be watchful and of any close family members who try controlling your life by playing with your mind.

Projecting: One of the common ways of manipulation in relationships is projecting. If you realize that your partner keeps on projecting their mistakes on you, the chances are that they are trying to control your life. Projecting is a situation where a person commits a mistake and tries blaming you for doing the same. For instance, if a person keeps on stealing your money and they start blaming you for stealing their money. This is often done to make the victim lose credibility. If the only person you are living with blames you of stealing their money, you will not be in a position to question them about your stolen money.

Deception: Another factor that shows that a person is trying to manipulate your life is lies. Try avoiding people who constantly tell lies about your life. A person who is manipulative will do anything possible to gain whatever they want from a relationship. If you are in a relationship with a manipulative family member, they will keep on lying and apologizing. The lies are geared towards making you give the other person your full trust. However, do not allow yourself to trust a person who does not tell you the truth. You should not pay attention to any person who uses trickery and other underhand methods to manipulate and control your life.

Dealing With it, and Fixing It

Although we allow toxic people in our lives, we are the ones who have a solution to every toxic relationship. It does not matter how long you have been together with a person. You must be in a position to deal with every toxic relationship and find a lasting solution. When you are in a toxic relationship with any person, you will end up on the losing side. Although the relationship may seem important at the beginning, you will end up experiencing losses in life. So how exactly do you deal with toxic friends and family members?

Confront them: If you realize that someone is the source of negativity in your life, you need to face them. If a person makes you lose confidence in yourself or they try manipulating you and use your resources for personal gain, you must stand up and face them. The fact that you can stand up and say no to the face of the manipulator gives you so much power. You should realize that the manipulative person has everything to lose in case the relationship comes to an end. If you stop such a person from controlling your life, it is easy for you to overcome any side effects of the manipulation.

Cut them off: In other cases, you simply have to stop supplying the manipulator with whatever is keeping them close. There are many instances where children take advantage of their parent's love and use manipulation to get money from parents. If you cut off such a person, they will have no other option but to walk out and try finding other means of earning. However, if you keep on feeding the manipulator with whatever they ask for, they will not stop asking. If a manipulative person asks for money and you keep on providing it, they will keep on increasing the amount they want. Before you know it, a manipulative person will completely drain your account and leave you with nothing.

Cut communication: The other option when it comes to dealing with manipulative individuals, is completely stopping communication. A manipulative person will continue coming to you if you give them an avenue to access your life. However, if you cut all avenues through which they may access your life, they have to stop. Manipulation starts to grow if you entertain all forms of social and family interactions with a manipulative person.

Conclusion

Congratulations on reading to the last page of the book. The fact that you were willing to read this book to the end shows your dedication and desire to gain knowledge on the subject of manipulation. If you have been keen, you have realized that dark psychology can affect any person. Whether you are young or old, you must equip yourself with some knowledge on the subject of dark psychology.

This book opens up your mind on the reality of the dark world in which we live. Although most people look good on the outside, there are many who plot evil against others. If you wish to protect yourself from all the dark aspects of life, you must learn to read people.

This book introduces you to the concept of dark psychology and how it works. The book further breaks down the subject and introduces you to the methods used in manipulation. An in-depth understanding of NLP and hypnosis will help you stay vigilant at all times. Further, this book teaches you the practical ways of reading people. You learn how to observe the thoughts of people and how to stop people from taking control of your life.

You are probably not sure how to start or where to start from in your quest to protect yourself from ark psychology. Given that the content of this book is wide, you must give yourself to learn the protection techniques one by one. A good starting place would be an in-depth understanding of NLP. As soon as you can read the thoughts of people using NLP, you will be on track to protect yourself and any person in your family from manipulation.

www.ingramcontent.com/pod-product-compliance
Lightning Source LLC
Chambersburg PA
CBHW072155020426
42334CB00018B/2020